The Gilded Age

CORNERSTONES OF FREEDOM™

SECOND SERIES

Ann Morrow

Children's Press®
A Division of Scholastic Inc.
New York • Toronto • London • Auckland • Sydney
Mexico City • New Delhi • Hong Kong
Danbury, Connecticut

Photographs © 2007: Art Resource, NY/The New York Public Library:
26; Bridgeman Art Library International Ltd., London/New York/Private
Collection/Peter Newark American Pictures: 14; Corbis Images: cover,
20 (Bettmann), 13 (Hulton-Deutsch Collection), 12 (Minnesota Histori-
cal Society), 40 (Perely Fremont Rockett), 3, 38, 44 top, 45 bottom;
Getty Images: 36 (Spencer Arnold/Hulton Archive), 7, 44 bottom (Solo-
mon D. Butcher/Hulton Archive), 27 (Hulton Archive), 28 (Mansell/
Time Life Pictures), 23 (MPI/Hulton Archive); Library of Congress: 18
(Lewis Wickes Hine), 19, 35, 39 (Kurz & Allison), 4 (Jacob A. Riis),
11 (Napoleon Sarony), 16, 22, 25; North Wind Picture Archives: 6, 24,
30, 31, 32, 45 top; The Image Works: 10 (Ann Ronan Picture Library/
HIP), 34 (Mary Evans Picture Library), 5 (Roger-Viollet/Topham).

Library of Congress Cataloging-in-Publication Data
Morrow, Ann, 1952–
  The Gilded Age / Ann Morrow.
      p. cm. — (Cornerstones of freedom, second series)
  Includes bibliographical references and index.
  Audience: Grades 4–6.
  ISBN-13: 978-0-516-23641-4
  ISBN-10: 0-516-23641-5
1. United States—History—1865–1898—Juvenile literature. I. Title.
E661.M65 2007
973.8—dc22   2006021097

CHILDREN'S PRESS, CORNERSTONES OF FREEDOM™, and
associated logos are trademarks and/or registered trademarks of
Scholastic Library Publishing. SCHOLASTIC and associated logos
are trademarks and/or registered trademarks of Scholastic Inc.

1 2 3 4 5 6 7 8 9 10 R 16 15 14 13 12 11 10 09 08 07

On a warm June day in 1893, "Diamond" Jim Brady sat down to eat lunch in one of his favorite New York restaurants. Brady had made a fortune with the New York Central Railroad, and he liked to eat well. He wore diamond rings, a diamond tie clip, and diamond buttons on his vest. He ordered his usual lunch of lobster, crabs, clams, oysters, beef, and several whole pies for dessert.

Jacob Riis took this photograph of a New York City tenement apartment.

In another part of the city, Jacob Riis, a Danish **immigrant** and photographer, snapped a startling photo in a New York **tenement** building. Twelve people, all of them immigrants, slept in one small room. Two or three were in bunks; the rest were on the floor.

In South Dakota, a Sioux Indian watched the sun set on the Great Plains. The vast herds of buffalo, which had once numbered in the millions, had dwindled to a few hundred. The best hunting lands were full of white settlers. Many in his tribe were sick and hungry.

In New Orleans, a black American family bought tickets for a trip on the East Louisiana Railroad. They walked past the cars reserved for "whites only" and looked for the cars marked "coloreds only." Under the terms of the Louisiana Separate Car Act of 1890, to do otherwise would mean a twenty-five-dollar fine and twenty days in jail.

All of these different scenes have one thing in common. They are images of the United States during the Gilded Age.

A boy sits on the ruins of a demolished church in Charleston, South Carolina, in 1865.

RECONSTRUCTION ENDS; THE GILDED AGE BEGINS

The Civil War, which began in 1861, ended in 1865 with the Confederate surrender to Union forces. The South was in ruins, with many homes, businesses, and railroads destroyed. This period after the war, known as Reconstruction, was a time to rebuild the nation. The **federal** government had to decide how to bring the former Confederate states back into the Union. It was also a time to find ways to protect the rights of slaves freed by the Emancipation Proclamation (1863) and the Thirteenth Amendment to the Constitution.

Members of the U.S. Congress await the electoral commission's decision on the winner of the 1877 presidential election.

CONSTITUTIONAL
AMENDMENTS

The Thirteenth Amendment

(1865) abolished slavery. The

Fourteenth Amendment (1868)

granted citizenship to former

slaves. The Fifteenth Amend-

ment (1870) guaranteed black

men the right to vote.

The Republican Party controlled Congress following the war and passed the Reconstruction Acts between 1865 and 1875. These acts granted some **civil rights** to freed male slaves and established military rule in Southern states until each state could form its own government. Congress also passed the Fourteenth and Fifteenth amendments.

In 1876, Republican Ulysses S. Grant was nearing the end of his second term as president. When it came time to find a new candidate for the presidential election that year, the Republicans nominated Rutherford B. Hayes, the governor of Ohio.

6

* * * *

After the election, a disagreement arose after the votes were counted. The Republicans believed Hayes had won the election. The Democrats, who had nominated Samuel J. Tilden, believed their candidate had the most votes. In January 1877, a fifteen-member electoral commission reached a **compromise** and awarded the presidency to Hayes.

To gain the approval of Southern Democrats, Hayes agreed to withdraw federal troops from the Southern states. This Compromise of 1877 ended Reconstruction and opened the doors to a new era known as the Gilded Age.

THE RISE OF JIM CROW

Many Southern states could not accept the idea that blacks who used to be slaves should have the same basic rights

A family of former slaves outside their Nebraska home

★ ★ ★ ★

as whites. These states passed their own laws that took away the freedoms granted to blacks during Reconstruction. These laws, which became known as Jim Crow laws, attempted to **segregate** black Americans and deny them equal rights.

While many former slaves remained in the South, large numbers chose to head west to escape racial **discrimination**. In the late 1870s and early 1880s, approximately 40,000 to 60,000 blacks moved to Kansas and western states in search of a better life and the chance to purchase land. Most were from Louisiana, Mississippi, Arkansas, and Tennessee. They were called Exodusters because large numbers made a mass exodus, or departure, at about the same time, from their home states.

RAILROADS: THE NATION'S FIRST BIG BUSINESS

Before the Civil War, railroads connected many cities in the East. However, most tracks went only as far west as the Missouri River. In 1869, the nation's first transcontinental railroad was completed. This new system crossed the continent and connected the eastern states with the rapidly growing western states. Growth of the nation's railroads quickly followed. Between 1871 and 1900, the nation's railroads grew by another 170,000 miles (273,500 kilometers). By 1900, five transcontinental railroads connected eastern and western states.

Trains could now transport people and goods quickly across the country. This replaced slower travel by steamboat and covered wagon and allowed settlers to move far from the rivers and roads they once depended on for transportation. Trains connected towns and settlements, and new towns sprang up as tracks extended their reach into undeveloped territory. Small businesses that once served customers in nearby communities now shipped goods around the nation. Inventions such as refrigerated railroad cars meant that farmers and merchants could rush their meat and produce to market before it spoiled. Sleeper cars made overnight train travel a comfortable option.

MONOPOLIES

The federal government did not run or control the railroads. Most were owned and operated by a small group of business-men. However, the states and the federal government recognized that railroads were important, so they provided money and grants of land to the railroads to keep them growing and to encourage settlement along their routes. The railroads sold some of the land to new settlers and made large amounts of money.

The railroads charged fees to merchants to ship their goods by train. Sometimes they charged differ-ent rates to different businesses, or offered very low rates to try to pull customers away from competing railroads. When one railroad took over all the other railroads in an area, it formed one large company, called a **monopoly**. Without competition, when a monopoly charged high rates, customers had no choice but to pay them.

"SEPARATE BUT EQUAL"

In a case known as *Plessy v. Ferguson*, the U.S. Supreme Court decided on May 18, 1896, that a Louisiana law requiring whites and blacks to use separate railroad cars was in keeping with the Fourteenth Amend-ment. This "separate but equal" policy sup-ported the Jim Crow segregation laws that required separate schools, water fountains, restrooms, and other services for blacks and whites.

The largest railroad companies became the first national businesses in the United States. Their owners grew very wealthy. While most Americans believed that railroads helped the nation grow, many were uncomfortable with owners holding so much money and power. They did not think it was right for big businesses to take over smaller companies to form monopolies and **trusts** that could charge high prices to customers.

Some Americans believed that the federal government should make one set of rules that all the railroads would follow. Some state governments passed laws to force the railroads to offer fair shipping rates, but it was clear that regulation had to come from the federal government.

In 1886, President Grover Cleveland and Congress passed the Interstate Commerce Act. It required railroads to publish their rates and file them with the government.

President Grover Cleveland

* * * *

Mines like this one in Minnesota grew after railroads made transporting goods and materials faster and easier.

The act created an Interstate Commerce Commission that investigated unfair shipping rates and other practices. The commission had the power to take railroads to court if they did not cooperate. Unfortunately, it often failed to enforce these new regulations or favored railroads over customers. Effective control of the railroad industry did not occur until after the Gilded Age.

THE RISE OF INDUSTRY

As the railroads grew, other industries grew with them. Mining companies used trains to ship raw materials such as iron, copper, silver, and oil to factories around the coun-

Andrew Carnegie

try. The factories then used railroads to ship the finished products to customers. The railroads themselves used large amounts of raw materials. Coal and wood fed their steam-powered locomotives. Miles of new rail lines required huge amounts of iron and wood.

Two industries that grew the fastest during the Gilded Age were iron and steel. They owed their success to the work of men such as Andrew Carnegie.

Laborers build a bridge that will be part of the transcontinental railroad through the Sierra Nevada mountains.

FROM RAGS TO RICHES

In 1848, when he was twelve years old, Andrew Carnegie moved with his family from Scotland to Pittsburgh, Pennsylvania. They hoped to find jobs and new opportunities in the United States.

Young Carnegie was energetic and **ambitious**. He soon found a job in a cotton factory, where he worked long hours for $1.20 per week. His money helped to support the family. Carnegie was a hard worker and looked for new jobs where he could earn even more money. By the time Carnegie was twenty-four years old, he was the superintendent of the western division of the Pennsylvania Railroad.

In 1865, Carnegie started the Keystone Bridge Company to build iron railway bridges to replace wooden ones. He bought iron mines and iron mills and invested money in oil. He knew that the new factories would need oil to run their machinery.

With the completion of the first transcontinental railroad in 1869, Carnegie realized that railroads would continue to be important to the growing nation. After a visit to England to observe the steel industry there, he saw new ways to make money. In 1873, Carnegie opened his first steel factory, the Edgar Thompson Steel Works in Pennsylvania. He later formed a huge corporation called the Carnegie Steel Company. Between 1881 and 1890, railroad owners bought almost 15 million tons (15.2 million metric tons) of steel rails and became some of the steel mills' most important customers. The manufacture of bridges, skyscrapers,

★ ★ ★ ★

and machinery also used large amounts of steel. By 1889, Carnegie was earning $25 million a year.

Carnegie thought that wealthy people should use their money to help others. He once said, "The man who dies rich dies disgraced." In his lifetime, he gave away more than $350 million. Carnegie believed that through education, people could learn to help themselves. In this spirit, he gave money to schools and founded more than 2,500 libraries throughout the world. His money also helped support scientific research, art, and music. In 1911, he formed the Carnegie Corporation of New York to give away his money after he died. The corporation continues to fund various causes today.

John D. Rockefeller

When Carnegie sold his business to banker J. P. Morgan for more than $400 million in 1901, his company was producing more steel than the entire nation of Great Britain. He was one of the richest men in the United States when he died on August 11, 1919.

ROBBER BARONS

Andrew Carnegie was not the only person to become rich during the Gilded Age. While he made his fortune in steel, John D. Rockefeller made his millions developing the Standard Oil Company. Cornelius Vanderbilt and Leland Stanford became wealthy railroad owners. Some people called these wealthy and powerful industrialists robber barons. They were accused of robbing the poor by making too much money, while those who worked for them made too little. Others thought of these men as captains of industry, smart and clever business leaders who provided new opportunities for citizens and immigrants.

In addition to railroads, steel, and oil, monopolies existed in tobacco, sugar, and other industries. In 1890, the federal government passed the Sherman Antitrust Act to make monopolies illegal. The act authorized the federal government to break up monopolies and trusts. It is still in force today.

THE NEW WORKPLACE

Much work of the large industries took place inside factories. This was a new work experience for most Americans who were used to running their own farms or small businesses and working on a product from start to finish.

Factories were often poorly lit, dirty, noisy, and unsafe. Machines quickly turned out goods once made by hand. Bosses, rather than workers, made the rules and set the production schedules. Jobs became monotonous, or repetitive and boring, as workers performed the same job throughout

CHILD LABOR

By 1900, about 1.7 million children under the age of sixteen worked in factories. Some states passed laws stating that children could not work more than ten hours per day. These laws were rarely enforced, and employers often ignored them.

the day. Wages were low, and work typically lasted ten to twelve hours a day, six days a week.

Accidents from unsafe conditions killed or injured hundreds of thousands of workers every year. The steel, mining, and railroad industries were particularly dangerous. Coal miners died from explosions and cave-ins. Machinery mangled, burned, and crushed industrial workers. Most companies did not pay medical bills for injured workers.

Some business owners put their desire for **profit** above concern for their workers. They did not want to spend money on improving work conditions. They also saved money by hiring women and children and paying them less than they paid men doing the same jobs. These bosses were not worried if workers quit their jobs. Plenty of other workers, many of them immigrants, eagerly took their places.

Knights of Labor leader Terence V. Powderly

STRIKE!

Workers unhappy with their jobs or workplace conditions often believed they had no choice but to endure the hardships. However, a growing number of workers joined labor unions, organized groups of workers who demanded change. The Knights of Labor, founded in 1869 in Philadelphia, Pennsylvania, was one of the first organizations to try to bring workers together. The Knights of Labor hoped to convince business and factory owners that a workday should be no more than eight hours. They also wanted equal pay for women, higher wages, safer workplaces, and an end to child labor.

19

Violence broke out during the strike at Carnegie's Homestead Steelworks in 1892.

* * * *

The unions had a powerful tool to use if employers ignored their demands. They could strike, or refuse to work. A strike involving many workers could completely shut down a business.

While some strikes during the Gilded Age were small, peaceful protests by workers, others turned violent. In 1877, several railroads cut wages. On July 11, railroad workers in West Virginia organized the first major strike in U.S. history. The strike soon spread to other cities. Strikers destroyed hundreds of railroad cars and miles of tracks. Trains stopped running in most of the eastern half of the nation. Finally, President Hayes ordered federal troops to move in. It was the first time in the nation's history that federal troops were used in peacetime.

By early August, federal troops had ended most of the strikes. Of the 10,000 workers who had gone on strike, more than one hundred were killed and 1,000 arrested. Some of the railroads agreed to listen to the workers' complaints, but change was slow to occur. However, the strikes taught employers and workers a valuable lesson: organized labor was a powerful tool for change.

Strikes and violent protests spread from the railroads to other industries in the 1880s and 1890s. Major strikes occurred in Chicago, Illinois, in 1886; at Carnegie's Homestead Steelworks in Pennsylvania in 1892; and in Pullman, Illinois, in 1894. When clashes resulted in death and injury, some members of the public blamed the organized labor movement. After the Chicago strike in 1886, membership in the Knights of Labor fell dramatically. Despite this, workers continued to organize throughout the Gilded Age. They formed other labor groups, such as the American Federation of Labor, the American Railway Union, and the United Mine Workers of America. Many of these labor groups are still powerful today.

IMMIGRATION

The United States had always been a nation of immigrants and an important destination for people from all over the world. In the nineteenth century, the numbers of immi-

European immigrants to the United States knew their long ocean journey had ended when they spotted the Statue of Liberty.

THE GOLDEN DOOR

**More than seventy of every
one hundred European immigrants entered the country
through New York City, which
some called the Golden
Door. In order to handle the
increase in immigrants during
the Gilded Age, the federal
government took over respon-
sibility for immigration from
individual states in 1891. An
immigration center on Ellis
Island in New York Harbor
opened on January 1, 1892.**

grants and their influence on the country became even
greater—nearly twelve million arrived between 1870 and
1900. Many came in search of jobs. Offers of free or cheap
land attracted others. Some hoped to find religious freedom
or to escape wars and violence in their own countries.

Until the 1890s, most immigrants were from Great Britain, Ireland, Germany, Norway, and Sweden. Large numbers
of them settled small farms or bought land from the large
railroad companies.

Near the turn of the twentieth century, immigrants started to arrive from eastern and southern Europe. Italians were the largest group, but there were also many Jews from Poland, Russia, and Romania, and large numbers of Slavs, including Ukrainians, Poles, Croatians, Czechs, and Serbs, among others.

Between 1880 and 1900, U.S. cities grew quickly, as large numbers of immigrants chose to settle close to the industries where they found jobs. This created a new set of problems for cities. They struggled to provide housing, water, sanitation, and other services for their residents.

A neighborhood of Polish and Russian Jews in New York City around 1890

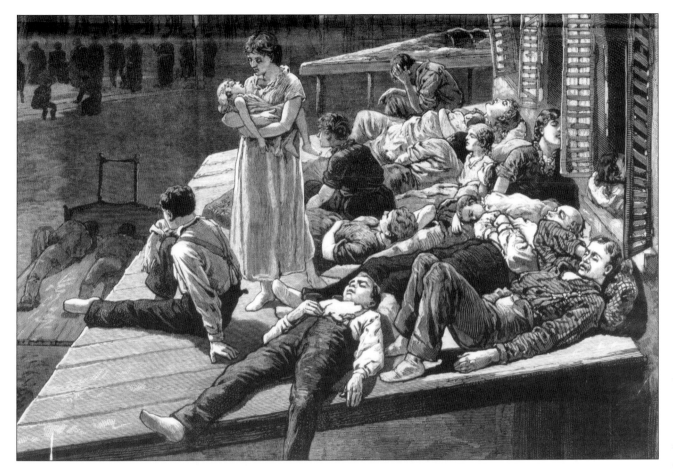

Many immigrants earned so little money that they had no choice but to live in tenements. After Danish photographer Jacob Riis visited a family of three in a tenement in New York, he wrote, "Their rent was eight dollars and a half [a month] for a single room on the top-story, so small that I was unable to get a photograph of it even by placing the camera outside the open door. Three short steps across either way would have measured its full extent." Sometimes families would take in **boarders** to help pay the rent. Tenements usually did not have indoor bathrooms or running water.

Tenements were so uncomfortable that many people slept on rooftops during the hot New York City summers.

The overcrowded conditions and poor sanitation made it easy for diseases such as cholera, typhus, and tuberculosis to spread. Many immigrant children did not attend school; they had to work to help support their families.

GOLD MOUNTAIN

On the nation's West Coast, thousands of Chinese and other immigrants entered California through the port of San Francisco after gold was discovered north of present-day Sacramento in 1848. The California gold rush began shortly after, and on September 9, 1850, California became

Chinese immigrants arrived in California looking for gold mountain.

Chinese miners panning for gold in California

the thirty-first state in the union. By 1851, 25,000 Chinese immigrants had moved to California, in search of *gam saan*, or "gold mountain."

Few miners ever actually struck it rich, and most Chinese miners did not find *gam saan*. Also, some American gold miners believed that Chinese miners were taking too much gold. The California legislature passed laws that prevented

Chinese miners from owning land or filing claims on land to begin mining for gold. It also passed the Foreign Miners Tax Law in 1852, which charged all foreign miners a monthly fee of twenty dollars.

By the 1860s, the Central Pacific Railroad needed workers to complete the western section of the first transcontinental railroad. Between 10,000 and 14,000 Chinese laborers filled these low-paying jobs. The work was difficult and dangerous. Many died as they blasted out tunnels with dynamite and built bridges through the steep Sierra Nevada.

A Chinese vendor stands beside vegetables, eggs, and spices for sale in San Francisco's Chinatown.

After the first transcontinental railroad was completed, there were fewer jobs for Chinese workers. Many wanted to return to China but did not have enough money. Some opened their own businesses or found work on farms in California. Because the Chinese were willing to work for low wages, some Americans believed the Chinese were taking jobs away from them. They wanted the federal government to stop the flow of Chinese into the country.

Denis Kearney, the head of the Workingmen's Party of California, led the battle against the Chinese. He believed that "California must be all American or all Chinese. We are resolved that it shall be American, and are prepared to make it so." He ended many of his speeches with the words, "The Chinese must go." In 1882, Congress passed the Chinese Exclusion Act. The law ended most Chinese immigration and prevented those who were already in the United States from becoming citizens.

NATIVE AMERICANS

To settlers who headed west in the nineteenth century, the land seemed vast and empty. Yet many Native American tribes had lived there for thousands of years. The Sioux, Cheyenne, Arapaho, Comanche, and others lived on the open grasslands known as the Great Plains. The Sioux were the largest and one of the most powerful groups. They were excellent horseback riders and hunted deer, antelope, elk, and buffalo.

Even before railroads crossed into the West, white settlers regularly passed through Indian lands on the Oregon, Boze-

BROKEN TREATY

The Treaty of 1855 set aside 7.5 million acres (3 million hectares) that stretched from Oregon Territory to Idaho Territory for the Nez Percé tribe. When a gold rush in 1863 brought thousands of settlers into Nez Percé territory, the federal government took back almost 6 million acres (2.4 million hectares) of this land.

Native Americans tried to resist the settlers, miners, and railroad builders who took over their lands.

man, and Santa Fe trails. The flow of travelers increased with the passage of the Homestead Act in 1862. This act offered 160 acres (65 hectares) to settlers willing to live and work on the land for five years. Native Americans resented the newcomers, who hunted the buffalo and settled on land the tribes considered sacred. The Sioux, Cheyenne, and Comanche mounted frequent attacks on settlements, stagecoaches, and wagon trains that invaded their territories.

As conflicts between whites and Native Americans increased in the 1870s and 1880s, the federal government signed treaties with many Native American tribes, forcing most of them to move onto reservations. This land was set aside just for use by Native Americans. However, both sides frequently broke the treaties, which resulted in increased hostility between the groups.

★ ★ ★ ★

By 1889, hunting by whites decreased the buffalo herds from several million to about 1,000.

EVERYDAY NEEDS

Native Americans used many parts of the buffalo to supply their daily needs. They boiled, roasted, and dried the meat. The hide provided clothing, tepee covers, and blankets. Buffalo bladders became water carriers; bones were made into weapons and tools; and glue was made from the hooves.

BUFFALO

For the Plains Indians, life revolved around the buffalo, which roamed freely on the Great Plains in large herds. Buffalo provided these Native Americans with most of their food, clothing, and shelter.

Surveys taken just after the Civil War estimated there were 10 million to 13 million buffalo in the country. The size of the herds decreased as interest in buffalo hunting by whites increased. Companies such as the American Fur Company offered money for the hides. Railroads provided an easy way to ship them to distant markets.

Buffalo hunters hired by the railroads further decreased the Plains Indians' main food source.

The railroads also hired buffalo hunters, such as William "Buffalo Bill" Cody, to kill buffalo to feed railroad workers. Some hunters killed hundreds of buffalo for sport and did not use the meat or hides. Others believed that killing the buffalo was a good way to starve the Native Americans by destroying their main food source. In 1866, General Philip Sheridan took over as leader of the U.S. forces in the West. He described his policy as, "Kill the buffalo and you kill the Indians."

By 1870, no buffalo remained on land east of the Missouri River. By 1889, only about a thousand remained in North America.

THE INDIAN PROBLEM

While some Americans thought that the best solution to the "Indian Problem" was to kill all the Native Americans or place them on reservations, others thought there was a better way. They called it **assimilation**.

They believed that the best way to get Native Americans to fit in to white society was to force them to adopt the ways of the whites. In 1879, Richard Henry Pratt founded the Carlisle Indian School in Pennsylvania, the first of many schools for Native American children. Pratt believed this was the best way to assimilate the Native Americans.

Native American children left the reservations when they were six or seven years old and returned when they were seventeen or eighteen. They had to cut their hair, speak English, wear American-style clothing, and learn the Christian religion. Those who returned to the reservations often felt like strangers within their own tribes and families. Many never returned home; diseases such as cholera, smallpox, and measles killed many students at the schools.

THE GHOST DANCE AND WOUNDED KNEE

In 1889, a Northern Paiute named Wovoka had a dream in which the Great Spirit appeared and told him that Native Americans could reach paradise if they lived peaceful lives and took part in a ceremony called the Ghost Dance. Other Native Americans thought the dream meant that the Ghost Dance would restore the Native American world to the way it was before the whites arrived and that the ghosts of dead ancestors would return. As word of Wovoka's dream spread, other tribes joined what became known as the Ghost Dance movement. The Ghost Dance gave the Native Americans hope that their lives would change for the better, but it was a concern to the U.S. government.

Worried that the Native Americans were planning to attack, the government ordered the arrest of Chief Sitting Bull at the

The Ghost Dance of the Sioux Indians

Standing Rock Reservation in South Dakota. During his arrest on December 14, 1890, gunfire broke out and he was killed.

Days later, a group of about four hundred Sioux Indians were returning to the Pine Ridge Reservation. The Sioux camped for the night at Wounded Knee Creek. In the morning, U.S. soldiers attacked, killing more than 250 Sioux. The Battle of Wounded Knee was the last major military action against the Native Americans. With the permanent loss of much of their traditional land, most Native Americans had no choice but to move onto reservations.

★ ★ ★ ★

The remains of the
battleship *Maine*, which
exploded in Havana harbor

AMERICAN EXPANSION

On February 15, 1898, the American battleship *Maine* exploded in the harbor of Havana, Cuba, an island in the Caribbean Sea about 93 miles (150 km) south of Key West, Florida. Two hundred and sixty men died in the blast. The cause of the explosion was never discovered. Many Americans blamed Spain, the country that controlled Cuba at the time. Cubans wanted to be independent from Spain, and the two countries fought over this issue from 1868 to 1878 and again from 1895 to 1898.

Americans took a great interest in the conflict because it reminded them of their own fight for independence from Great Britain, the Revolutionary War (1775–1783). In 1896, the Spanish military had rounded up 300,000 Cubans and forced them to stay in overcrowded, dirty camps. Thousands of women and children died of disease and starvation. This angered Americans. They wanted to help Cubans. War against Spain seemed like the only way. After the *Maine* incident, newspaper headlines, politicians, and other war supporters rallied Americans to the cause with the reminder, "Remember the *Maine*!"

President William McKinley did not want to go to war with Spain. He believed that **diplomacy** would offer a more peaceful solution. Theodore Roosevelt, the assistant secretary of the navy, disagreed. He believed that McKinley's position on the issue showed weakness. Many Americans agreed with Roosevelt. They thought it was time for the United States to show the rest of the world that it was a powerful nation. One of the ways to do this was to have territories in other parts of the world. On April 25, 1898, two months after the *Maine* exploded, McKinley declared war on Spain, and the Spanish-American War began.

Spain controlled not only Cuba, but also Puerto Rico, Guam, and the Philippine Islands. The first major battle of the Spanish-American War took place in the Philippines. On May 1, Commodore George Dewey destroyed ten Spanish ships in Manila Bay. In June and July, U.S. forces captured Santiago, Cuba. The U.S. Navy destroyed Spain's ships in the waters between Cuba and Jamaica, and U.S. troops captured Puerto Rico.

During the naval battle in Manila Bay, the U.S. fleet destroyed Spain's Asian fleet.

Theodore Roosevelt (center) led a famous cavalry unit in the Spanish-American War.

AFTER THE WAR

Cuba gained independence from the United States in 1934. Hawaii became the fiftieth state in the union in 1959. Independence was granted to the Philippines in 1946. Today, Guam is a U.S. territory and Puerto Rico is a **commonwealth** of the United States.

On August 12, the war ended when Spain surrendered. The war had lasted only four months. Nearly 275,000 U.S. military had served in the war, and 379 had died in battle. A far greater number—5,462—died from yellow fever, malaria, and other diseases that were contracted from insect bites in the dense rain forests of the **tropical** climates.

Tropical diseases were a bigger threat to U.S. troops in the Philippines than battle death or injury.

Now that the United States had control over the Spanish colonies, it had to decide what to do with them. Some U.S. leaders wanted to add the lands to the United States. Others thought doing so would be against the nation's democratic principles. The debate was ended on December 10, 1898, when Spain and the United States signed the Paris Peace Treaty. The United States paid $20 million to Spain and took control of Cuba, Puerto Rico, Guam, and the Philippines.

Next, President McKinley and Theodore Roosevelt, who had served in the Spanish-American War, turned their attention to the Philippines. They believed that by controlling Hawaii, which became a U.S. territory in 1898, and the Philippines the United States could become a powerful force in the Pacific Ocean and Asia. However, like the Cubans, many Filipinos wanted their independence. American and Filipino forces fought over this issue from 1899 to 1902. When the conflict ended, more than 4,200 Americans and 18,000 Filipinos had been killed. Disease and starvation had killed another 100,000 Filipinos. The Philippine Islands were again a territory of the United States, which controlled land from the western Pacific Ocean to the Atlantic Ocean. The United States had proven that it was a world power.

THE AGE OF REFORM
The Gilded Age was a time of great change that brought the nation growth in population, industrial strength, and military power. It also brought the nation a new set of problems. How should society deal with immigrants, black Americans, and Native Americans? Was it possible to be fair to business owners and their workers at the same time? How should the country deal with friends and enemies overseas?

During the last decade of the Gilded Age (1890–1900), many people worked hard to find answers to these questions and to find ways to improve American society. They turned their attention to child labor laws, immigration, poverty, woman suffrage (the right to vote), and racism. These progressives, as they called themselves, continued their work after the turn of the twentieth century. The Progressive Era, which followed the Gilded Age, continued until World War I (1914–1918).

Glossary

ambitious—having a strong wish to be successful

assimilation—the process of one race or culture absorbing the ways and traditions of another

boarders—people who pay to live in a place and receive meals

civil rights—privileges, such as the right to vote, that belong to citizens of a country

commonwealth—a nation or state that is governed by the people who live there

compromise—an agreement in which each side gives up something it wants

diplomacy—the practice of conducting respectful discussions between nations in order to avoid hostility

discrimination—prejudice or unjust behavior toward others based on differences in age, race, gender, or other factors

federal—having to do with the central government in Washington, D.C.

immigrant—someone who leaves one country to settle permanently in another

materialism—a way of living in which a person places a high value on money and possessions

monopoly—the complete control of something, especially a service or the supply of a product

profit—the amount of money left after the costs of running a business have been subtracted from the money earned

segregate—to separate people, particularly based on race, class, gender, or ethnicity

tenement—a rundown apartment building, especially one that is crowded and in a poor part of a city

tropical—relating to the extremely hot, rainy area of the earth near the equator

trusts—groups of companies that form one powerful corporation that acts as a monopoly

Timeline: The Gilded

1865	1869	1873	1877

1865

The Civil War ends with Union victory and Reconstruction begins.

Andrew Carnegie starts the Keystone Bridge Company.

1869

The Knights of Labor is established in Philadelphia, Pennsylvania.

The nation's first transcontinental railroad is completed.

1873

Andrew Carnegie opens his first steel factory.

1877

Rutherford B. Hayes becomes president after an election dispute.

Reconstruction ends and the Gilded Age begins.

Violent railroad strikes paralyze the nation's rail system.

Age

Richard Henry Pratt establishes the Carlisle Indian School in Pennsylvania.

The Chinese Exclusion Act is passed by Congress.

The Sherman Antitrust Act is passed by Congress.

More than 250 Sioux are killed by U.S. soldiers at Wounded Knee.

A violent strike occurs at Andrew Carnegie's Homestead Steelworks.

Immigration center opens at Ellis Island.

The Spanish-American War begins and lasts four months.

The United States takes control of Hawaii, Cuba, Puerto Rico, Guam, and the Philippines.

The Gilded Age ends and the Progressive Age begins.

To Find Out More

BOOKS

Fremon, David K. *The Jim Crow Laws and Racism in American History*. Springfield, N.J.: Enslow Publishers, 2000.

Halpern, Monica. *Railroad Fever: Building the Transcontinental Railroad 1830–1870*. Washington, D.C.: National Geographic Children's Books, 2004.

Landau, Elaine. *The Wounded Knee Massacre*. Danbury, Conn.: Children's Press, 2004.

ONLINE SITES

The Library of Congress: America's Stories—The Gilded Age
http://www.americasstory.com/cgi-bin/page.cgi/jb/gilded

New Perspectives on the West
http://www.pbs.org/weta/thewest/program/

U.S. History for Kids
http://pbskids.org/wayback/index.html

Index

Bold numbers indicate illustrations.

About the Author

Ann Morrow has been a freelance writer in Florida for more than twenty years. Her writing has appeared in a variety of books, magazines, and newspapers. This is her first book for Children's Press.